POSITIVE COACHING
In a Nutshell

Jim Thompson

A distilled rendition of the coaching classic

Positive Coaching:
Building Character and
Self-Esteem through Sports

D1712266

Warde Publishers Inc.
Palo Alto, California

Warde Publishers, Inc.
530 University Avenue, Suite 102-7
Palo Alto, CA 94301
(800) 699-2733

FIRST EDITION
Printed in the United States of America
10 9 8 7 6 5 4 3 2 1   10 09 08 07

Contents

"Start a huge foolish project like Noah.
It makes absolutely no
difference what people think
of you." —Rumi

This book is dedicated to the early adopters
who transformed Positive Coaching Alliance
from a foolish project into a huge movement.
It may make absolutely no difference
what I think of you, but—for the record—
I think you are terrific.
—Jim Thompson

In a Nutshell

The playing field is the ideal place to teach life lessons and positive character traits. It is a virtual classroom with an unending procession of teachable moments, if we look for them.

Positive Coaching: From Book to Alliance

I thought writing *Positive Coaching: Building Character and Self-Esteem Through Sports* would change the world and I'd get back to my "normal" life. Instead it changed my life. I was drawn into the fascinating world of youth sports and never got out.

In 1998, I moved from Stanford's Graduate School of Business to Stanford's Department of Athletics to start Positive Coaching Alliance (PCA). PCA has grown into a nationwide movement to transform the culture of youth sports that has benefited millions of youth athletes.

Not in North Dakota Anymore

The changes in youth sports remind me of Dorothy in *The Wizard of Oz*: "I don't think we're in Kansas anymore, Toto."

My first experience as a youth coach in Palo Alto, California in the mid-1980s was shocking to someone who had grown up playing baseball, basketball and football in small towns in North Dakota. There hadn't been that many adults involved in our makeshift games on the sandlots of Colfax, Galchutt, Walcott, Wyndmere, Mayville and West Fargo. And the games were fun! Sometimes they went on until it was too dark too see or until we were so hungry we had to go home to refuel.

By 1985, youth sports had become an adult-organized activity with a lot of unhappiness and stress on kids, parents and coaches. Like Dorothy, I realized after getting a taste of this brave new world, "I'm not in North Dakota anymore."

Now things have deteriorated further. Positive Coaching Alliance compiles an annual list of the "Bottom 10 Moments in Sports" (available at www.positivecoach.org). Too many of the terrible incidents are from youth sports.

The Good News

But there's good news. PCA partners with hundreds of schools and youth sports organizations (YSOs) across the U.S. Our corps of dynamic trainers deliver live workshops all over the U.S. and Canada. And demand for PCA's program is growing.

A Difference You Can See

Organizations that implement the PCA program are different. The organizational culture they create is visibly different from the win-at-all-cost nastiness too often prevalent today in youth sports. Taking a "systems approach," Positive Coaching culture starts with organization leaders who are committed culture shapers. Leaders articulate a clear vision of "Double-Goal Coaches®" who try to win (goal #1) while pursuing the second goal of using sports to teach life lessons. Parents are "Second-Goal Parents" who let athletes and coaches try to win while they help their child take away from sports lessons that will help them be successful in life. When the adults in youth sports are on the same page, sports is a beautiful and enriching experience for everyone involved.

PCA's 10-minute DVD, "Honoring the Game," available from PCA's online store at **www.positivecoach.org**, is great for parent meetings to let them see what a positive youth sports culture looks like.

Why This Book

This book—a distilled version of the original *Positive Coaching* —emerged directly from PCA's work with youth sports organizations and schools.

People are busy. And youth sports leaders and coaches are among the busiest. A "nutshell" version of *Positive Coaching* allows coaches to read it in a sitting. It also lends itself to organizations buying one for each of their coaches to help create a strong Positive Coaching culture. (Bulk discounts and customization editions are available from Warde Publishers at www.wardepub.com, 1-800-699-2733.)

I hope many readers of this nutshell version will decide to read the original version with its many stories and elaboration of the ideas and tools presented here. But for those with little time to spare, this nutshell version is for you.

Join the Movement

Positive Coaching Alliance has a mission to transform youth sports. But we can't do it alone. If you like what's in this book, get involved. Become a PCA member, and get certified as a Double-Goal Coach. As a member, you'll be able to keep up with PCA's growth through our newsletter, *Momentum*, and our electronic newsletter, *PCA Connector*. Encourage schools and youth sports organizations you know to partner with PCA. Spread the word. With your help, we're going to change the world!

PCA offers workshops for youth sports leaders, coaches, parents and high-school age athletes. To find out more about these live and online workshops, check the PCA web site at **www.positivecoach.org** or call (toll-free) 1-866-725-0024.

Chapter 1

Teachable Moments Through Relentless Positivity

It is the relentless commitment to positive coaching that brings success. It's when things go wrong that you can have the biggest impact, if you can continue to be relentlessly positive.

It is assumed that if taught properly, the athletes will learn. But the hidden part of the iceberg is the receptivity of the learner. Learner receptivity is captured beautifully in the phrase "teachable moments," those timeless times when athletes are focused on what they need to do to improve. How do you produce the highest number of teachable moments for your athletes? Let's begin with relentless positivity, the cornerstone of great teaching because it leads to teachable moments.

The Case for Positive Coaching

Here's why positive coaching works better than negative coaching.

1. **The greatest coaching principle in the world**: Michael Leboeuf in *The Greatest Management Principle in the World* says: What gets rewarded gets done. Encourage your athletes to do good things and they will try to do them again.

2. **The futility of punishment**: Punishment eats away at motivation. When kids are punished or yelled at, their emotional energy is used up being angry, feeling sorry for themselves, thinking up reasons why the coach is wrong, etc. Punishment may stop behaviors, but rarely leads to new ones. It takes positive reinforcement and recognition to get a child to try something new, such as fielding bad hops without turning his head. Dolphin trainers rely exclusively on positive reinforcement. Punishment doesn't work with dolphins. They withdraw and refuse to perform. Kids are like dolphins. Positive works better.

3. **Responding to a challenge:** Challenges require emotional support. Without support a child's energy goes to defending himself against real and perceived criticisms from others. When a child knows that he will be valued and accepted by his coach and parents, *no matter how he performs*, more of his energy goes to responding to the challenge.

The Emotional Tank is a key concept in getting kids to improve. Everyone has an E-Tank like the gas tank in a car. When your E-Tank is empty, you can't drive very far. When a child's E-Tank is empty, you are not going to get his best effort. You can read more about the Emotional Tank on pages 61–100 of my book, *The Double-Goal Coach*.

Positive Charting

A corollary to the greatest coaching principle in the world is: **People do what gets measured**. Positive Charting addresses what you want your athletes to do. Here's how to do it.

1. Write each player's name with space to comment on an 8.5 × 11-inch piece of paper.

2. During a game or practice, jot down positive things each athlete does. Make sure you have about the same number of items for each player (3–5 is good).

3. Be honest. Don't make things up. Look hard and you will find positive things that each player does.

4. Start the next practice with a quick team meeting to share your comments with your team. Each player gets 30 seconds or so of the spotlight.

5. Enjoy the positive energy of your players now that you've filled their E-Tanks!

The Magic Ratio

Research shows about five E-Tank fillers per criticism is optimal for motivation. Keep track of tank-fillers and criticisms during a practice with pluses and minuses on paper (or your hand!). You'll be amazed at how many criticisms you hand out. Once you get up to 5:1, you'll see why it's called the Magic Ratio. Your athletes will be so pumped they'll do things that you would have thought impossible.

Non-Teachable Moments

Some moments are just not teachable.

1. **Games**: In general, games are for implementing things already taught. There is so much tension in any closely contested game, that players won't have emotional energy to learn something new. Note things in games that you want to teach at the next practice and focus on filling E-Tanks during the game.

2. **Mistakes**: When a child makes a mistake that may cost her team the game, she knows it. The last thing she needs is to be yelled at. Even criticism gently offered right after a mistake may be hard to take in her embarrassment. Wait to give that feedback!

3. **When you are angry**: Kids won't respond well to criticism when you are angry. Call a break, have an assistant take over, work with another kid. Wait for your anger to subside before you try to instruct the player again.

4. **Factors beyond your control**: Sometimes players come to practice with drained E-Tanks because of happenings at home or school. In these situations, kids are not going to have as many teachable moments. All you can do is be as positive as you can to try to refill the child's E-Tank.

Acceptance Time

Acceptance time is the time it takes to process criticism and embrace it as one's own. Some changes take longer than others. Teachable moments are not always flashes of breakthrough. They can be an accumulation of small interactions with players that create an atmosphere in which learning and growth take place. Give athletes time to process criticism and feedback. It will pay off.

The Discipline of Positive Coaching

There is nothing tough about getting negative when things go wrong. Any toddler throwing a tantrum is "tough" in that sense. A truly disciplined coach provides emotional support to a player who has just blown a play that cost a game. Mental toughness is remaining positive in the face of adversity.

Teachable Moments Through Ideas and Inspiration

Ideas are the great motivator. Human energy is released by the right idea at the right moment. But the best idea can't inspire unless properly communicated.

Coaches can exploit the power of ideas through *stories, metaphors* and *vision*.

The Coach as Storyteller

Humans respond to stories. Great coaches collect stories to help players make sense of what can seem a series of random events.

Stories that give players perspective: Tough situations can be transformed by the right story. I once coached a baseball team playing for the championship on a very hot day. Players complained about the heat. I could almost hear their inner dialog: "We shouldn't have to play when it's so hot. No one can expect us to play well today."

I shared a basketball game growing up in North Dakota. Late in the game with Valley City High School, I was exhausted as

I ran the floor. However, then I noticed the player guarding me was breathing heavily. Realizing he was also tired inspired me. I felt a surge of energy and sped past him to score. I concluded by telling my players: "Today is hot for *both* teams. If you guys hustle, you can demoralize them. They'll be thinking about how hot it is, and you'll make it worse by out-hustling them." We won the game handily, with no more complaints about the heat.

Practice, Practice, Practice: Isaac Stern was asked how to get to Carnegie Hall. He replied, "Practice, practice, practice."

To inspire players to work hard, I share Bill Bradley's end-of-practice routine from John McPhee's book, *A Sense of Where You Are*. At Princeton, Bill Bradley stayed after every practice until he made 10 of 13 shots from every spot he might shoot from in a game. I told them Bradley was not blessed with great strength, speed or leaping ability. But he became an All-American and professional star because he worked to improve those parts of his game that he could control. Bill Bradley's 10-for-13 practice regimen gives young players a powerful tool to improve their shooting.

Cutting Through the Noise with Metaphors

Lots of distractions or "noise" compete with the coach for kids' attention. That's where similes and metaphors can help. Similes use "like" while metaphors compare two unlike things implying that the two things are the same.

> Simile: "He runs like a gazelle."

> Metaphor: "He is a gazelle out on the field."

Move Like a Monkey: I was having trouble getting my beginning basketball players to shuffle their feet on defense. They got tangled up when their man changed directions. I began scratching under my arms and making monkey sounds as I shuffled my feet. The kids thought it was hilarious and began to mimic me! From there on, when I saw players running when they should have been shuffling, I yelled out "Monkey" and they would immediately shuffle their feet.

Watering Tomato Plants: I tell players they can't reach their potential if they work on their sport only at practice. "In practice we plant tomato plants. But plants need constant watering. To be a great player, you need to water your tomato plants outside of practice." From then on, all I had to do is ask, "Have you been watering your tomato plants?"

Ropes and Little Steps: Once on a ropes course, I was asked to scale a 30-foot pole, climb a 12-inch metal platform at the top (that rotated!), stand up and leap to grab a ring dangling a few feet away. (I was belayed by rope so the only danger was in my head—although it didn't seem that way!)

I climbed the pole and peered up at the ring, which seemed far out of reach. An instructor yelled to me that I didn't need to catch the ring. All I needed to do now was get my right foot up on the platform. What happened next was the stuff of a peak performance testimonial. Calmness came to me. I breathed deeply and spent some time looking at the beautiful forest around me. I put my right foot up on the platform, paused and breathed. I brought my left foot up, paused and breathed, then let go of the platform. Slowly I straightened up and stretched out my arms.

Amazingly, the platform did not shake. The thought came into my head: "Hey, I can reach that sucker!" I leaped and grabbed the ring with my right hand, to the roar of friends below who had silently urged me on each step of the way.

I shared this "little steps" story to help my team to concentrate on the next little step facing them, rather than jumping ahead to look at a ring that was discouragingly far away.

PCA's *Coaching the Mental Game* workshop uses the power of ideas to help athletes deal with pressure. It introduces visualization and other tools to reframe situations to help athletes control their performance. Information is at **www.positivecoach.org.**

Vision: Seeing the Opportunity

Jerry Porras and Jim Collins, authors of *Built to Last*, define vision as the ability to see the possibility in a situation. There is *always* the possibility of something better occurring, no matter how bleak it appears. Here are some examples.

The All-Star Trouncing: A Little League all-star team I was coaching got way behind in the first inning of the first game of a double-elimination tournament. By the second inning we were behind 12-0. The mood in the dugout needed to improve a lot before you could say it was somber.

To get players focused on the opportunity in the situation, I asked them to tie or win *this* inning. Behind 15-0, even that may not have seemed possible, but in the fourth inning, we tied them, 0-0. The fifth inning was a decisive victory, 2-1. We also tied the sixth, 1-1. Observers who arrived in the 5th inning might have thought we were wining by the way our dugout was cheering, our batters were aggressively going after the other team's pitcher, and the hustle shown by our fielders.

We lost 17-3, but then won two games before being eliminated on a bad-hop grounder in an extra-inning game. That team then lost 1-0 in three extra innings to the team that beat us so badly in the first round. The momentum that carried us successfully through the rest of the tournament was generated in the last three innings of our blow-out loss.

The Expansion Team: A friend managed an expansion baseball team. With one experienced player, the coach realized the chance for a winning season was not good. He gave the team a realistic (but challenging) goal. No expansion team had ever won more than three games. He told them that they could be the best expansion team ever if they won four games. He also said that they had a good chance at winning the league championship the following year.

The team lost most of its games, but the players were up for every game. They surpassed the goal with five victories and went on to win the championship the next year. And it started with seeing the possibility in a 5–19 season.

The Outfield Rules: I was assistant coach on a strong baseball team with a terrible outfield. I offered to work with the outfield to give us a better chance at the championship.

Our outfielders were discouraged. They knew they were the weak link, and that other players resented them for always screwing up. They were disheartened and needed to be pumped up. I held special practices "just for the outfielders."

My initial motivational speech: "The other teams have kids playing the outfield who don't want to be there. They don't realize the outfield is the key to winning the big games. All the teams have pretty good players in the infield. But we can be the only team that also has a great outfield. When you play against the better teams, they hit more balls to the outfield! In the big games, the outfield is the key to winning."

Our outfielders began playing with pride, and improved even more than I could have hoped for. In a key game, Jeff, our centerfielder, staggered up against the fence and caught a towering drive, like "a prizefighter who had taken too many blows to the head," in the words of one parent. Another time Brian chased down a foul fly after a long run from left center field. Matt caught three fly balls in a row, more than he had caught the entire season up to that point.

Seeing their potential turned this group of kids into a tough group of fielders who helped win a championship.

Where Energy Comes From

Human energy comes from emotions which are released by ideas. Coaches who want to increase teachable moments will tap into the power of ideas via stories, metaphors and vision, to motivate their athletes.

Chapter 3

Teachable Moments Through Engagement

Kids learn best when engaged in the learning process. Coaches increase the number of teachable moments by putting players in charge of their own learning.

Expecting Kids to Think

Many coaches seem to want players to be highly responsive robots, which hardly prepares them for situations where there's no coach to tell them what to do. Coaches should look at sports as an opportunity to develop thinking skills, and that starts with *expecting* kids to think. Set the expectation from the first day of practice that you expect them to use their heads on the court or field.

Thanks for Not Listening to Me

A favorite memory from coaching very young baseball players was when a player made a difficult throw from third base to second to get the lead runner, while I was yelling for her to throw to first base. I learned two things from this: I try not to yell directions at players when a play is going on; and when I forget and a player makes a play contrary to my instructions, I say "Thank you for *not* listening to me."

Asking Rather Than Telling

Coaches have thousands of opportunities to tell players what to do. Resist this temptation and look for opportunities to *ask* your players what they should do—this will improve their decision-making over time. If a player makes a "wrong" decision, go over it with him later to help him understand a better decision for the situation. You can also keep players on the bench engaged in a game by asking them questions: "What did Kristin do on that play that made it work?"

Coaches who look for chances to increase players' thinking skills will find an inexhaustible source of opportunities to ask questions in every game.

Getting Kids Teaching Each Other

We often think we know something until we try to teach it, when we discover we don't understand it so clearly. It's when I teach someone else that I really learn it. So, get kids to teach each other to increase their understanding of their sport.

Incorporate Kid-Teaching Into Your Teaching: When you teach a new skill, ask players to teach each other. Here's how:

1. Explain and demonstrate how to do the skill to the entire group.

2. Ask players to pair up to demonstrate to each other how to do the skill.

3. Encourage them to encourage each other as they work together.

4. Wander to observe who needs your feedback and instruction. By giving advice in private, the players will be more open to it than if given in front of everyone.

5. Ask for volunteers to demonstrate the skill in front of everyone.

Train Kids as Teachers: Improve the impact of Kid-Teaching by working with selected player-teachers on a skill beforehand. This can give veteran players a leadership role, but I recommend eventually letting everyone do it. Less talented players will advance more quickly as they become teachers themselves.

Whose Goals?

People work incredibly hard when motivated from the inside. Often coaches impose goals with little player buy-in. Instead suggest goals to players. If they say "Yes," you have buy-in. Also ask players to set their own goals so they will be more motivated to achieve them. If players pick unrealistic goals, help them pick interim goals that are achievable so they don't get discouraged.

PCA's live workshop *The Double-Goal Coach: Winning & Life Lessons* shows how to have kids set "effort goals" (that are within an athletes reach if she works hard) and "stretch goals" (that require effort over time to reach). You can read about them on pages 42-51 of my book, *The Double-Goal Coach* or through PCA's online workshop at **www.positivecoach.org.**

Workers Rather Than Products

Ted Sizer noted in schools where kids get excited about learning, the "central metaphor is student as worker rather than student as product." Get athletes excited about learning by getting more of the "work" produced and directed by them. The best coaches are developers of people as lifelong learners.

Chapter 4

The Coach's Role in Increasing Self-Esteem

Our self-worth depends upon our perception of how important others value us. For a youth athlete, the coach is one of the most important individuals in his or her life.

Self-esteem is one's internal judgment of oneself. Individuals with high self-esteem are glad to be who they are. They are comfortable in their own skin.

The Language of Self-Esteem

A child who believes he isn't good at baseball, but learns to improve, can make the same leap in other areas. "Speaking Chinese is hard but I can learn to do it!" The language of self-esteem is encompassed in two phrases:

"I can **do** this!" and

"I can **learn** to do this!"

A coach who reinforces the use of these phrases, who shows players they can **do** and **learn to do**, is giving them a great and lasting gift, the belief they are strong enough and smart enough to handle whatever life throws at them.

PCA's workshop for high school athletes, *Becoming a Triple-Impact Competitor*, teaches that a "Teachable Spirit" is central to becoming a great competitor. An athlete with a Teachable Spirit is a sponge who just can't get enough knowledge about her sport.

Self-Worth and Important Others

At Camp Owendigo in Minnesota, Don Challman told me, "It's not your job to be liked by the kids. Your job is to like them."

I want to be around people who like me because they make it easier for me to like myself, take risks and make efforts necessary for growth. Most of us can't develop a healthy sense of self-worth by ourselves. We are social creatures, and we derive our feelings about ourselves from how we perceive *important others* treat us.

Notice it isn't how others value us, but our **perceptions** of how they value us. If someone thinks highly of me but never communicates it, I do not benefit. As a coach the key is to **communicate** that you accept and value them in ways they can't mistake.

The Emotional Tank

How to Really Love Your Child, by Ross Campbell, first introduced me to the "Emotional Tank" in each of us. When treated in ways that make us feel valued, our E-tanks fill. Negative stuff drains our E-tank. Children are more likely to try new things and make efforts with full tanks. When their E-Tanks run down, kids tend to withdraw, or "act out" and become behavior problems (See Chapter 14 for behavior problems).

How to Fill Emotional Tanks

Here's a list of ways coaches can fill E-Tanks of athletes.

1. **Names**: It's said that what most people want to see in a newspaper is their own name. Every athlete should be greeted and bid farewell by name. Hearing their names spoken in a friendly tone of voice is music to players' ears.

With a new team, I use the "Name Game" at the first practice. We form a circle and I start: "My name is "Coach Thompson and my favorite baseball player is Roger Maris." The next player introduces me to the rest of the team, "This is Coach Thompson and his favorite player is Roger Maris. My name is Jason and my favorite player is Darin Erstad." And so on.

2. **Smiling**: Many coaches act as if too much smiling is unsportsmanlike. Smiling at players is an easy way to let them know you value them.

3. **Joking**: Humor that doesn't make fun of someone causes people to enjoy each other's company, which is important in the often stressful setting of a team.

4. **Eye Contact**: Friendly eye contact communicates caring.

5. **Appropriate Touching**: Touching kids needs to be appropriate, but tousling a player's hair, patting players on the shoulder, exchanging high-fives, etc. communicates that you like and value your players.

6. **Influence-ability**: I know I'm important to others if I have influence with them. Ask players advice about what to do in a given situation, which says you care enough to ask them what they think. Players often want to play a

position beyond their ability. View blowout games as chances to give kids a chance to play their favorite position, and let them know they have influence with you.

7. **Listening**: There are times when a coach has to make a decision the athlete is not going to like. But it helps to give the child a chance to say his piece. Listening without interruption communicates caring and that you take them seriously. Sometimes that is more important than the specific problem a player is upset about in the first place.

8. **Apologies**: When adults apologize to children for a mistake they make, it sends a powerful message of caring. A coach who finds the humility to apologize to a player is communicating in a direct way that he values the player.

9. **Forgiving**: We forgive because we care about people. Often coaches take it personally when a child misses practice, or fails to execute a play. Being able to forgive and move on is an advanced skill for a coach.

10. **Asking for Help**: Coaches fill E-Tanks by asking players to help. Being asked for help signals to players that they are important members of the team and is a big E-Tank filler.

11. **Appreciation and Recognition**: When someone notices our effort, we want to make more efforts. Here are guidelines for recognition and appreciation:

    a. **Accuracy**: You may have to search for something to say about your weakest player, but resist the temptation to make something up that isn't true to make her feel better.

    b. **Behavior-specific**: Saying "Great job!" is okay. But it's much more powerful to say, "Way to block out for that rebound!" Positive Charting (Chapter 1) gives you raw material with which to recognize your players.

c. **Tie to Goals of the Team**: Tying the efforts of each individual to the success of the group helps build a team. You can add to the example above: "Way to block out for that rebound! That helped keep us in the game."

d. **Written is Better than Spoken**: People recognize it takes more effort to write a note of appreciation, and they value it more. The written word has staying power whereas spoken statements fade over time.

e. **Avoid Humor in Recognition**: I've learned not to be funny when recognizing players. People take recognition of themselves very seriously (even if they don't show it). Making a joke can tarnish the recognition moment.

12. **Bragging**: Bragging about someone conveys pride in that person. Kids need to be bragged about by important persons in their life. As a coach, I try to tell parents something good about their child's play every time I see them.

13. **Individual Teaching Time**: Single players out for individual teaching time. Don't spend all of your teaching time with the most talented players. Taking time to work with less talented players on an individual basis is a big E-Tank filler.

14. **Negative Feedback Gently Delivered**: Athletes often get yelled at when they make a mistake. A gentle word about how they might improve can be the stimulus to improve where yelling mainly allows an undisciplined coach to vent.

15. **Helping See One's Potential**: Many adults tell me how a coach helped them see potential they were unaware of. A coach is often in a better position to do this than a teacher or parent. Most of us would work so hard for someone who helps us see our potential.

16. **Photographs**: I make a point of taking lots of photos of my players. The very act of asking them to stand still or pose for a photo sends a message of caring.

Self-Endorsement: The Ultimate in Self-Esteem

No one can always be in a supportive environment. Highly competitive elite sports, can be cutthroat. Kids need tools to endorse themselves when they are in an unfriendly environment. Ask athletes how they felt about their performance rather than always telling them your view. Being able to endorse oneself when others are critical can only be helpful to their future success. And that is what youth sports should be all about.

Chapter 5

The Opportunity to Build Character

Kids don't pick up positive character traits by osmosis. Coaches need to seize the normal, stressful, day-to-day situations of sports to teach athletes positive character traits.

The Coach's Most Important Character Trait

The #1 character trait of an effective coach is the ability to be there for your athletes. It's so easy to let the desire to win or look good cause you to do something harmful to the development of your players. No matter how badly things go in a practice or game or season, by supporting your players, you can help them draw useful conclusions from what happens to them.

"Character-Building Time"

In adversity lies the potential for development of mental toughness and other positive character traits. Help athletes develop character when they face a difficult situation by saying, "It's character building time! I'm glad you're in this jam. That's the only way you'll ever learn to work yourself out of one!"

Character-Building Traits

Decide which character traits are important to you. Some possibilities.

1. **Mental Toughness**: Mental toughness is suffering discomfort to accomplish something important to you. When players are in a tough spot, tell them it's an opportunity to develop mental toughness. Their performance will improve as they focus away from fear of failure to working on developing mental toughness.

2. **Having Fun**: Being able to enjoy challenges makes for happier, more successful people. Successful people enjoy what they do and put more energy into solving problems and less into worrying. Talk about how much you enjoy challenges and ask players if they are having fun, especially during trying times. Help them see challenges as opportunities to be relished rather than things to be feared.

3. **Winning and Losing with Class**: Teach players that class means never sacrificing principles to win. Ask them to not show glee when an opponent fails. Encourage them to help opponents up after a collision. Insist on a rousing cheer for the opposing team every game, win or lose. Point out examples of classy behavior whether by your team or the opposing team.

PCA's evolved version of sportsmanship is the ROOTS of Honoring the Game: respect for **R**ules, **O**pponents, **O**fficials, **T**eammates, and **S**elf. Organizations that partner with PCA make Honoring the Game a central part of their culture. See pages 101–145 in *The Double-Goal Coach* for more on Honoring the Game.

---

4. **Courage**: Courage isn't the absence of fear—it's doing what is right or necessary in spite of the fear. If you're not afraid, you can't be courageous. Encourage your athletes to see scary situations as opportunities to develop courage.

5. **Setting and Commitment to Goals**: While most people wait for others (teachers, parents, coaches) to tell them what to do, successful people set their own goals. Help athletes set goals. Ask them what they want to get better at and what they want to accomplish. Have them come to the next practice with their goals. Help them develop a plan to achieve their goals. Ask players often how they are doing with their goals. If they are having trouble, encourage them to re-establish more realistic goals.

The Centrality of Effort

William James noted that the only thing we bring to our life is the amount of effort we put into it. Everything else—our physical talents, our personality, our family's wealth—are given to us. But what is up to us is how hard we try.

Tell your players that, more than anything else, it is the amount of effort they are willing to put into their sport that determines how good they can become. Recognize gritty efforts by your players. If you do, you'll teach them a valuable lifelong lesson about the centrality of effort.

DIMITT

Teach DIMITT ("Determination is more important than talent!") to athletes to reinforce the notion that they will be just as good as they are determined to be.

Teaching Positive Character Traits

Teach positive character traits as you would teach any skill.

1. Introduce and define character trait #1.

2. Emphasize the trait throughout the season.

3. Look for stories to share with your players that illustrate that trait.

4. Recognize players when they demonstrate that character trait.

5. Repeat for character traits #2, 3, 4, etc.

Teaching Character After the Season is Over

Point out character development during the season at your end-of-season party (see Chapter 15). Mention each player's character development as well as skill development and other contributions to the team. Sometimes players listen to you more closely then than during the entire rest of the season. Send them off to the rest of their lives with kudos for the positive character traits they developed on your team!

Chapter 6

Making the Most of Mistakes

Fear of making a mistake is a paralyzing force that robs athletes of spontaneity, love of the game, and a willingness to try new things. When a coach accepts mistakes as part of the learning process, athletes gain the psychological and emotional freedom that unlocks the learning process and occasionally releases truly inspired performances.

The Lifeblood of Learning

Mistakes are the lifeblood of learning. In *Self-Renewal*, John W. Gardner noted that without the willingness to make mistakes, learning shrivels up.

"One of the reasons mature people are apt to learn less than young people is that they are willing to risk less. Learning is a risky business, and they do not like to fail. In infancy, when children are learning at a phenomenal rate—a rate they will never again achieve—they are also experiencing a great many failures…by adolescence the willingness of young people to risk failure has diminished greatly. And all too often parents push them further along that road by instilling fear, by punishing failure or by making success seem too precious."

I am forever indebted to Sister Grace Pilon who, in her "Work-shop Way," taught that only humans make mistakes because it takes intelligence to make a mistake. Over and over, Sister Grace would say, "It's okay to make a mistake." I have tried Sister Grace's mantra with many kids. The initial reaction is slight, but when the first athlete makes the first mistake, the magic words hit home. A woosh of held breath signifies a release of tension when the player realizes that this coach will not come down on her for making a mistake.

A "Mistake Ritual" helps players bounce back quickly from mistakes. Players flush mistakes down the toilet using a flushing motion with their hand to help refocus on the next play. More on mistake rituals is on pages 51–56 in *The Double-Goal Coach*.

Mistakes and Concentration

A player worrying about making a mistake is not concentrating on doing the job.

Once when I was coaching tee-ball, a boy named Ivan was having a terrible time hitting the ball in a game. Even though the ball was stationary on a tee, Ivan twice missed it completely. I called time and whispered to him. He went back to the plate and smashed the ball for a triple. Ivan's dad asked me, "What did you say to him?" I had simply asked Ivan if it was okay for him to make a mistake. He nodded his head, relaxed, and went back and powered the ball, as he was capable of whenever he focused on the task rather than on whether he would fail.

Mistakes and Effective Effort

A coach who makes it okay for players to make mistakes will get more effort from them than a coach who reacts to each mistake like it is the end of the world.

Most kids have what Rudolf Dreikurs, in *Children: The Chalenge,* called "mistaken goals." As coaches, we think our players' goal is to make the play. But often, they are simply trying to avoid looking stupid. No one wants to look bad in public, and few things are as public for a youth as a sports contest.

I once saw a shortstop gracefully lope after a pop fly. He looked great but he didn't get there in time to make the catch. I told my players he was so concerned with looking graceful he didn't make the play. From then on I encouraged my players: "Make the play and don't worry about looking graceful." Often a gritty effort would be met with "Way to **not** be graceful," from coaches and players.

Mistakes and Substitutions

When you remove a player immediately after a mistake, you are saying it is *not* okay to make a mistake. If you don't want your players holding back from fear of mistakes don't substitute for a player right after she makes a mistake. Some coaches, about to sub a player out, will delay that action a few minutes because they don't want any of their players to think they will get pulled for a mistake.

When the Coach Makes a Mistake

We once lost a game when the umpire incorrectly called the infield fly rule on a pop-up that bounced foul before any fielder touched it. We would have won the game if we coaches had had the wits to protest the call (respectfully, of course!). We began the next practice by apologizing for making a mistake that cost us the game. Our players immediately said, "It's okay to make a mistake, coach!"

The Same Mistake Again and Again

A repetitive mistake is a symptom not the real problem. A runner who leaves 3rd base early on a fly ball may need to be taught to look the ball into the outfielder's glove before heading home. He may fear contact at the plate. Whatever the problem, a repetitive mistake is a clue to help you correct it with the athlete.

Mistakes and Winning

But don't mistakes lead to losing? John Wooden, one of the winningest coaches in history: "The team that makes the most mistakes will probably win…the doer makes mistakes, and I wanted doers on my team—players who made things happen."

Where Good Judgment Comes From

My boss at the Oregon Department of Energy, Lynn Frank, used to say whenever he or I screwed up, "You get good judgment from exercising bad judgment." As coaches who want to use sports to develop young people of character, we need to learn to make the most of mistakes.

Chapter 7

Making Practices Productive (and Fun!)

Nothing drains the excitement and wonder out of youth athletes quicker than being forced to stand around at unorganized and unproductive practices.

Practice is critical. It determines how a team will play.

The Habit of Over-learning

Athletic contests are most often determined by athletes' *habitual* responses. There isn't time to think things through. You make a decision or the moment for a decision passes. It doesn't even seem like a decision—you just react.

The only way to learn a skill well enough to use in the heat of a pressure situation is to over-learn it and that takes repetition. Effective practices get kids the repetitions they need to make the appropriate response a habit.

Make a Commitment to Learn

Effective practices take commitment and hard work. Make a commitment to organize the best practices you can.

PCA provides numerous resources to help you be a better coach: an ever-expanding collection of materials, including an online Double-Goal Coach workshop at **www.positivecoach.org**.

Being Prepared (In Writing)

Thinking and writing are inextricably bound together. So, "think it and ink it," and write out your practice plan.

Most of my practice ideas come from games—things that need work identified in previous games or to prepare for upcoming games. Unless I write these ideas down, I usually lose track of them before I can incorporate them.

I may not know what to cover in the next practice, but if I start writing, ideas come to me and the practice is better than if I wing it. A poor written plan is better than an ideal plan that exists only in my head. So write it down!

Share Your Plan with Your Team

Post on the wall or give your players a copy of the practice plan at the beginning of practice to let them know what you will cover that day. Ask for their best effort, which will increase the likelihood of a great practice.

Building Around a Core

It's hard to come up with a unique plan for every practice, so I structure practices around a core, which keeps me focused and reduces wasted energy. Players learn the routine and require less explanation.

Core practice activities are covered in PCA's workshop *The Double-Goal Coach: Culture, Practices, and Games*:

- Objectives and priorities
- Opening ritual
- Instruction
- Skill drills
- Conditioning
- Emotional Tank Filling
- Scrimmages
- Team conversations
- Closing ritual
- Assessment

The First Practice of the Season

Expectations are set at the first practice and can be difficult to change once set in players' minds. At my first practice I tell players I am excited about coaching **them**, that I want **them** on my team.

The Big Three and Rule Number One

I then talk about the Big Three goals and Rule Number One.

"Goal #1 is to have fun. If you're not having fun, you won't play your best! Goal #2 is to try our hardest. Trying hard and having fun are entwined so if we try hard, we'll have more fun and we'll do better. Goal #3 is to be a good sport. I want you to be a good sport win or lose. Now these three goals together are difficult. Any one of them alone can be easy. It's easy to be a good sport if you don't care about winning. It's easy to have fun if you win all the time, but I want you to have fun and be a good sport even when we lose.

"Rule Number One on this team is that it's okay to make a mistake. You can't learn anything new without making mistakes. I want each of you to learn a lot this season and that means that you will make a lot of mistakes, and that's okay."

Developing Control with a Gentle Hand

Young athletes are like horses. They want to run free and feel the wind in their manes after being in the stable (school) all day. They want to *go* someplace and *do* something. They also don't want to be totally on their own, they want guidance and structure. And the best guidance is a gentle hand. Coaching with a gentle hand requires confidence you can tighten the reins when you want control, which comes from reinforcing the behavior you want.

Reinforcing behavior you want: When players do what I ask, I thank them. When they don't, I ignore them so as to not reinforce the undesired behavior. This works like magic because kids respond to attention, even negative attention.

If I yell at Billy for not coming when I call, it may reinforce his behavior. When a player comes right away, I say, "Thank you, Joe, for coming when I called." When Billy realizes he is not getting my attention—and Joe is—he usually behaves so he can get my attention, and the only way to get it is to do what I ask.

Once players understand they get my attention by doing what I ask, they work hard to get it. That allows me to coach with a gentle hand knowing I can get their attention when I want it.

Pacing and Variety: Mix up practice activities so players get a change of pace. Hold team conversations following a running activity so tired players will be more attentive to what you say. Use the pattern of teach–drill–scrimmage so players don't have to sit listening for a long time before they get to try the skill and use it in a game-like situation.

Most coaches talk too much (including me!). Make your talks short and sweet and punctuate them with drills, competitions, water breaks, scrimmages, etc. The less you talk at any one time, the more likely your players will hear you.

Fun and Drama at Practice

If practice isn't fun, few kids are going to improve much, nor are they going to keep playing the sport. Here are four ways to get more fun into practice.

1. **Competition (with or without handicaps)**: Scrimmaging almost always makes practice more fun.

Small-sided games get everyone involved. In baseball a game of "work-up" can involve several teams of 3 or 4 players who bat while the other teams of players take the field. The at-bat team bats until they make three outs, then they take the field and the next team in the rotation goes to bat. In basketball you can run a mini 3-on-3 tournament.

Handicaps add to the fun. Play soccer with only the weak foot allowed. Play basketball with no dribbling allowed. Play baseball with any ball hit on the shortstop side of the field counted as an out (this helps players learn to place the ball). More competition usually means more fun.

2. **Reduce the Level of Play**: Temporarily reducing the level of play adds fun and motivation to a practice. Older baseball players love hitting off a tee. Shorten the playing field in soccer to increase the intensity and fun.

3. **Have Coaches Play**: This is fun for players but take care to avoid injury. Bigger, stronger coaches can hurt younger players. Coaches with bodies older than their competitive spirit can get seriously injured if they compete with young athletes the way they did when they were young.

4. **Bring Drama into Practices**: My wife used to show up at the end of practice with ice cream. (She also sometimes brought our three pugs to practice and the players would go nuts as the dogs chased them around the court.). Some coaches have "slurpee drills" in which players who catch a fly ball, for example, get treated after practice (this works best when everyone qualifies!). I've used special jerseys that players "earn" by a desired behavior in practice (e.g., helping out on defense to prevent a score). Once one of my players said, "But everyone will try to help out on defense so they can wear the jersey." Yes!

Delegating to An Assistant Coach

Here are ways to delegate to increase learning in practice.

1. **See & Do**: Have your assistant watch you teach a skill and replicate it with another group of players.

2. **Plan & Preview**: Ask your assistant to plan to teach a specific skill at an upcoming practice. Ask him to preview it with you before trying it out on the players.

3. **Do & Report**: Ask your assistant to teach a skill to part of the team, while you work with the rest. Ask your assistant to report how it went and anything she would do differently next time.

If you have no assistant, Chapter 3 shows how to get players to teach each other.

PCA has developed a Mentor Coach workshop to teach experienced coaches how to be mentors to their assistants and other young coaches. Check the PCA web site to find out more about it at **www.positivecoach.org**.

Show Your Players How the Big Guys/Gals Practice

Take your players to see a practice of a local college or high school team. Most college and high school coaches are happy to have you observe, and many will let their players talk with yours afterwards. This can be very inspiring for young athletes who want to play in high school or college.

Chapter 8

Coaching in a Game

Games are different. How kids perform in games matters more than practice, and they know it.

The Coach As Cheerleader

Athletes are psychologically vulnerable in games (their mistakes are on display for all to see). Be their biggest cheerleader. Let them know you support them NO MATTER WHAT, so they don't waste their energy worrying you will go negative on them.

Coaching Up to the Kids

My high school basketball coach DeWitt Batterberry noted that coaches he admired "coach up to the kids." What a great phrase! Be a coach who coaches up to your players so they play up to their potential.

The Thrill of the Crowd and Teachable Moments

Playing before an audience enhances the performance of athletes who know how to do something well, while degrading the performance of athletes who haven't mastered something.

Teachable moments are rare in a pressure-filled game and it is a rare athlete who can learn something new during a game (as opposed to the lower-pressure and more private environment of a practice session). Because of this, I tend not to teach new things during a game. I do record things players need further work on during the next practice for later conversation about how we can prepare to address problems in the next game.

Preparing Your Team for Games

Coaches who prepare players fully for the challenge of a game will find their players can't wait for a game so they can rise to the challenge. Here are some ways to prepare for a game.

1. **Have a Game Plan**: A bad written plan is better than no plan. Write your plan down to help you deal with your anxiety so you can focus on helping your players.

2. **Make Adjustments**: Don't get so tied to your game plan that you aren't able to adjust when things don't follow the plan. Some tips:

   a. **Prepare Mentally**: After you have done all your preparation, sit quietly for 15 minutes to get yourself mentally ready for the challenge of coaching a game.

   b. **Anticipate the Opposition**: What does the other team do well, poorly? Where are we most vulnerable? How can we adjust to that? Where is the other team vulnerable? How can we take advantage of that?

   c. **Adjust to Officiating**: Focus on how officials are calling the game (e.g., the ump is calling lots of strikes.) Tell players what you've noticed to help them adjust to the officiating.

   d. **The Final Adjustment**: Sometimes you plan well but it doesn't turn out well. Be prepared to lose gracefully, in a way you can be proud of, and feel good about having prepared the best way you knew how.

3. **Pep Talks**: Youth athletes seldom need to be "psyched up" before a competition. Instead, focus their attention on the game plan. "We've been practicing all week for this so let's review what we are going to try to do today." Share tips about the opposition. "Number 25 is very aggressive on the boards, Ricky and Jason, so you're going to have to block out big time!" Finally, remind them that this is a game and games are supposed to be fun. "Let's give it our best effort and have fun playing today!"

Helping Players Deal with Pressure

Here are two ways to help players deal with pressure.

1. **Nervous is Normal**: L.A. Lakers star James Worthy said, "I like to be a little bit afraid, to be nervous. It usually conjures up some good energy." Tell players nervous is normal. If they aren't a little nervous, they won't have energy to play their best.

2. **Give Them Something to Focus Their Nervous Energy on**: We can learn from *mahouts* in India who give an elephant a bamboo shaft for its trunk so it won't eat bananas it passes in the market. Give athletes tasks to complete early in a game when nervousness is high: a set play to

start a game or a phrase to say silently during their first shot. It's hard to think of two things at once, so give them something positive to focus on to combat nervousness.

Teaching Character Behaviors in a Game

Games offer countless chances to teach character lessons. Share **specific behaviors** you'd like to see in games. Tell players you'll know they can win and lose with class when you see them:

- Wish their opponents good luck before a game.

- Congratulate opponents when you lose and thank them for a good game when you win

- Seek out officials to shake hands and thank them (even if the official made calls that went against them)

When you see these behaviors, tell them they are making you proud to be their coach.

The Missing Element in Most Games

In a win-at-all-cost society, fun often goes missing in sports. So before every game, remind them to have fun!

Chapter 9

Handling Parents

More than any other factor, it's parents that give coaches pause. However, when properly managed and appreciated, parents can become a potent partner in getting the best from players and building a great team.

The Sources of Parental Misbehavior

There are several sources of sports parent misbehavior.

1. **Distorted Perceptions**: When we want something we become susceptible to distorted perceptions. An official's call against our team will be seen as wrong when we want to win so badly. Distorted perceptions by parents who want their children to do well are normal! You can defuse misbehavior by your parents by saying to them, "I didn't like that call, but, I think it was correct."

2. **Reliving Past Glory**: Some parents have experienced glory as athletes, most have not. Either way, there is a tendency for parents to get more excited about their child's game than anything else in their life.

3. **Boundary Confusion**: Many parents believe other people judge them by how well their child does in sports. They

forget they are not their child—that their child is a separate human being with his own abilities and short-comings. Telling parents you won't blame them for anything their child does can help calm them down.

PCA's online *Second-Goal Parent* workshop (**www.positivecoach. org**) helps parents help their child get the most from sports. Encourage your parents to take the online workshop or get your organization to offer a live **PCA** workshop for parents.

Getting Parents on Your Side

Here are some simple things to do to get parents on your side.

1. **Keep them informed**: Parents have a lot going on. Make life easier for them: let them know when practices begin and end, the upcoming schedule, and any information that makes their overscheduled lives easier. If you say practice will end at a certain time, make sure it does.

2. **Tell them good things about their child**: Find something truthful and specific to say to parents about their child every time you see them.

3. **Get their kids in the game**: Parents want to see their child play! Play each kid as much as you can. Many coaches play weaker players the bare minimum even in games that are decided early. Look for chances to play weaker players and you will make their parents very happy.

4. **Fill parents' Emotional Tanks**: Chapter 4 lists ways to fill E-Tanks of players. Use those tools to make parents feel part of the team experience, because when their E-Tanks are filled, they'll be better able to fill their child's E-Tank.

PCA's "Road Map to Excellence" for PCA partner organizations, includes a downloadable Parent Letter and a Parent Pledge that commits parents to not coach from the sidelines. Go to **www.positivecoach.org** and search for "Road Map" for both.

Guidelines for a Coach-Parent Partnership

Here are guidelines for getting parents to be your partner.

1. **Don't put the player in the middle**: A parent who complains about you to his child is undercutting your ability to be successful with him. Ask parents to come to you if they have questions or problems, rather than criticizing your coaching in front of the child.

2. **Ask for feedback**: Encourage parents to tell you anything that might impact their child's performance. I once had a boy with a severe hearing loss whose parents never mentioned it. I got so frustrated with him, many times I had to restrain myself from yelling at him, "Are you deaf?"

3. **No instructions from the sideline**: Tell parents you often have kids work on specific things during a game and they can interfere if they yell instructions. Ask them to cheer, but to let you do the coaching.

4. **Fill their child's Emotional Tank**: Tell parents to emulate parents of Olympic athletes—they are their child's biggest fan and cheerleader. Ask them to fill their kid's E-Tank regularly and often.

5. **Be part of your team's "Home Team Advantage"**: Ask them to fill E-Tanks of all your players. Explain that teams play better at home because of the support of the crowd,

and that you want to be able to make that home team advantage a portable one for your team.

6. **Respect the other team**: Ask them to show the utmost respect for the other team even if the other team is not respectful to us. Ask for their help in building a team that wins and loses with class.

PCA has a job description for parents as "Culture Keepers" who encourage parents on the sideline to Honor the Game. Ask a parent to be your team's Culture Keeper. Go to **www.positivecoach. org** and search for "Culture Keeper."

Enlist Parents in Character Development

Ask parents to help. Tell them that when things go wrong, they can help by reinforcing resiliency, determination and a can-do attitude with their child. Tell them they can also help their child develop these character traits by repeating again and again that they love and are proud of their child no matter how they perform.

Chapter 10

What About Winning?

Sometimes when we coach to win, we do worse than if we come at winning indirectly.

In this society, winning seems to be everything. "Professional" coaches brutalize players, display an atrocious lack of sportsmanship, and throw tantrums like three-year-olds. Yet this behavior is tolerated *as long as they win*.

What Did Vince Lombardi Mean?

What did Green Bay Packers coach Lombardi mean when he said "Winning isn't everything, it's the only thing?" Did he mean it is okay to:

- Cheat to win?

- Risk the health of players to win?

- Overlook a violation of a team rule or substance abuse by a star to win?

- Neglect one's family responsibilities to win?

You can instantly get in a ferocious debate with Lombardi fans or critics on this, but the more crucial question is how important is winning to **you**?

In the heat of decision-making in a big game the line between acceptable and unacceptable behavior blurs. You can't always rely on your judgment at crunch time if you haven't been clear with yourself about how important winning is to you.

The Power of OPO

One reason coaches, in the heat of competition, act in win-at-all-cost ways is because of the power of OPO—other people's opinions.

Unless you coach in a program partnering with PCA (perhaps even then), people tend to evaluate you as a coach by win-loss record. No matter that you seize teachable moments to teach life lessons, get reluctant players to improve, and have practices kids can't wait to come to, if you don't win, many people will conclude you aren't that great a coach. It's normal to worry about what others think of you, but you can lessen the power of OPO by writing down what you will and won't do to win.

It's hard for coaches in a win-at-all-cost culture to be Double-Goal Coaches (who want to win and teach life lessons). PCA's workshop, *Leading Your Organization: Developing a Positive Coaching Culture*, shows how to create an "educational-athletic organization" rather than a mini-professional league. Youth sports organizations (YSOs) can earn the *PCA Seal of Commitment* by committing that every one of their coaches will be trained and certified as Double-Goal Coaches. Information on the *PCA Seal of Commitment* is at **www.positivecoach.org**.

Write It Down

It really helps to write down what you are willing to sacrifice to win, and what you are **NOT** willing to do. It is especially important to write down goals that may, in fact, make it harder to win (e.g., getting your weaker players playing time).

For example, are you willing to:

- Play only your better players to win?

- Encourage your players to bend the rules?

- Spend time planning practices so they will hum?

- Work with weaker players outside of practice time to help them improve?

- Work hard to learn more about coaching your sport?

Take out pencil and paper and start writing:

- To help every player on my team have a terrific season, I will . . .

- Even if it means losing a game I really want to win, I will **not** . . .

- To become the best coach I can be, I will . . .

The Paradoxical Impact of Positive Coaching

We've all tried to remember something to no avail, only to recall it when we turn our minds away from it. Sometimes the quickest way to a goal is indirectly, like looking away slightly to see a particular star.

When your overriding goal is to build character and self-esteem, you sometimes find that you win *more* that you expect to. In Chapter 12, you'll find that kids with increased self-confidence try harder and stick to a task longer. And kids who are having fun with a sport practice longer and more often. And those are the elements of a winning effort.

Learning From Losing

Losing is an important part of sports and life. If we want to use sports to teach life lessons, we need to value losing for the lessons it can bring our players and us.

Thomas Edison tried more than 1,000 times to invent the light bulb before success. Had he been in a competitive young inventors league, he likely would have been branded a failure and become discouraged long before the light bulb came to be.

A win-at-all-cost mentality makes it easy to overlook important lessons to be learned from losing. For example, it is difficult to develop persistence in the face of adversity without the adversity. You can't keep getting back up if you're never knocked down. It's hard to rebound after a loss if you never lose.

A Kid's Perspective on Losing (and Winning)

As a coach eloquently put it, "Losing sucks. Winning is more fun than losing."

Losing often is more painful for coaches than players. Once in a serious funk immediately after losing a close game, I noticed my players chattering about their plans for the rest of the weekend. Unlike me, they were not at all depressed.

Tom Tutko told of talking in the car with his son after a losing soccer game. Being a sport psychology professor, Tom thought he needed to say something profound to his son. "You know that 50% of the teams that play soccer always lose?" No response. "I remember when I was young, I played in a game I really wanted to win, and it really hurt when we lost." At this his son slid over in the seat and put his arm around his father saying, "It's okay, Dad." At that point Tom says he knew that one of them was severely disturbed.

When Things Go Wrong

Coaches who want to make a positive difference in their players' lives should welcome adversity. Once when one of my basketball players got into a fight after a hard foul, I was devastated and took it as a personal reflection on my coaching. But it became an opportunity to work with two young men with great potential (as athletes and human beings). Both boys got sage advice and support from several different adults. Both understood that this behavior was not acceptable. They shook hands and apologized, and life went on with no further incidents.

It's important to remember that it's when things go wrong that coaches can have the most impact.

Getting Back Up

A scene in the movie *Gandhi* serves as a metaphor for mental toughness. Gandhi calls a demonstration at which Indians in South Africa are to burn their identity cards. As Gandhi sets fire to his card, a policeman knocks him down with a club. Gandhi gets up and returns his card to the flame. Again the policeman knocks him down, this time harder. Again, Gandhi gets up. Each time as Gandhi rises, more Indians, initially fearful of joining the protest, approach the fire with their cards.

The real test of character is not whether we occasionally get knocked down, but how many times we get back up. A great thing about youth sports is that athletes can get knocked down without getting knocked out. With a supportive coach, a knockdown can help kids become the kind of person who gets back up, as good a definition of a winner as I can imagine.

PCA's ELM Tree of Mastery redefines what it means to be a winner in terms of mastery rather than the scoreboard. ELM stands for Effort, Learning, and responding to Mistakes. A player who gives her best effort, continues to learn and improve, and bounces back from mistakes is a winner, regardless of the score! More on the ELM Tree of Mastery on pages 17–60 of *the Double-Goal Coach*.

The Loose Freedom of the Underdog

As quarterback for the West Fargo High School (ND) Packers, we played an exceptionally strong Fargo Shanley team ranked number one in the state. The *Fargo Forum* ran an article about our game saying, "Can the Packers beat Shanley? Will the sun rise in the west?"

We couldn't make the sun reverse direction but we did play a terrific game. I threw three touchdown passes as we came closer to beating Shanley than any other team that year.

Because everyone expected us to be crushed by Shanley we loosened up and played our best game of the season. That was my first experience of the loose freedom of the underdog, a rarified state where losing isn't something to be feared.

A Final Reason for Appreciating Losing

Near the end of *The Hobbit* by J.R.R. Tolkien, Gandalf says to Bilbo Baggins, who is confused about the adventure he has just participated in. "'You don't really suppose, do you, that all your adventures and escapes were managed by mere luck, just for your sole benefit? You are a very fine person, Mr. Baggins, and I am very fond of you; but you are only quite a little fellow in a wide world after all!' 'Thank goodness!' said Bilbo laughing...'"

Winning can do strange things to our heads and our sense of balance. Losing restores us to balance. Losing helps us realize there is more to life than what goes on between the first and third base lines. We coaches, whether of children or professional athletes, are really just quite little fellows (and fellowettes) in a wide world after all. Losing helps us remember that.

Chapter 12

Nurturing Outstanding Individual Competitors

Outstanding competitors are driven by internal motivation. Coaches can reinforce the attitudes and behaviors of great competitors in all their athletes, but should **not** use rewards and punishment in ways that undercut internal motivation.

Here are five crucial characteristics of great competitors.

1. **Internal Motivation**: Great competitors are motivated more by internal goals than by external rewards such as money or status. Internal passion for the sport unleashes super performance. Michael Jordan said, "I love the game for the game, not just for the money. If I wasn't getting paid, I'd still be playing the game of basketball somewhere. A lot of people don't understand that."

And a lot of coaches don't understand that fear and greed aren't as powerful motivators as joy and love of a game. To develop advanced skills, an athlete has to *like* to play the game. You don't acquire the highest level of skill without an incredible amount of practice. Most people aren't willing to put in the amount of practice time needed to develop high-level skills unless they enjoy the activity.

Sometimes coaches will try to increase a player's motivation by giving them external rewards. Unfortunately, "carrots and sticks" tend to undermine internal motivation. Instead of more total motivation, you simply exchange precious internal motivation for less valuable external motivation.

People tend to look for reasons for their behavior. When a player is not getting paid or rewarded externally, he concludes that he works hard because he loves it. When external rewards enter the picture, he may now conclude that he is doing it for the rewards, and then slack off when the rewards lessen or go away.

External rewards can boomerang, and coaches are wise to help athletes develop their own motivation rather than relying on external rewards. As my friend Paul Solomon once said, "It's hard to be driven when you are being driven."

2. **Energized by Challenges**: Outstanding competitors relish challenges. They want to be on the spot at the end of the game—to shoot free throws with no time on the clock, to try to drive the ball past the goal keeper in the shoot-out.

Psychologist David C. McClelland noted that different people have different needs: for affiliation with other people, for power, for achievement. People with high need for achievement work to create challenges for themselves. When tossing rings over a peg, they place the peg just far enough away to be a challenge. People with less need for achievement place the peg so close they are assured of making it, or so far away there is little chance of hitting it.

In general, outstanding competitors want to compete at a level that will push them to be their best, not at a level where they can succeed without risk. They respond to a challenge with greater effort and are energized by it.

3. **Seeing Development as Under Their Control**: Many youth athletes believe that athletic ability is fixed—you either have it or you don't. Either way, there is not much they can do to increase their ability to play the game.

Competitors see their development as a process they control. If weak at a skill, they know they can improve by practicing and they work at it until they do. If they can't do a skill, they know they can learn it if they work at it.

People who are not great competitors attribute their failure to bad luck or lack of talent. Great competitors attribute success and failure to their own efforts rather than the hand that life or genetics has dealt them.

4. **Decision-makers Rather than Order-takers**: Most coaches *say* they want their players to be good decision-makers, but coaches often reinforce dependency in their players. Often practices seem like dog training sessions rather than a process to develop young people. Outstanding competitors tend to be independent and willing to challenge conventional wisdom.

5. **Accepts Success and Failure**: Outstanding competitors can deal with success and failure. Because they do not fear failure, they focus their energies on trying to win and never play "not-to-lose."

Athletes often fear success. Success leads people to expect more success. It is easier to be an ordinary athlete than a great one, if everyone expects you to be great all the time. Who needs that kind of hassle? Competitors do not let fear of success keep them from reaching their potential.

What Coaches Can Do

Here's are some guideline for nurturing great competitors.

1. **Teach Internal Motivation**: Tell athletes that for them to be the best they can be, they need to be internally motivated. Let them know they're more likely to become great athletes if they love the sport and have fun with it. Encourage them to work hard because they choose to do so, not just to please you.

2. **Teach Skills as Acquirable**: Tell about players you've coached who weren't initially successful at a skill but who with practice learned to do it. Share your experience of practicing something you thought was impossible, until you got it. Collect stories of great athletes who improved because they practiced.

3. **Provide Mastery Experiences**: There is a story about a farm boy who could lift a huge cow. Asked how he got so strong, he said he started when the cow was a newborn calf. He lifted it every day, and since the cow's growth was gradual, he was able to lift it every day with just a bit more effort. Break key skills into pieces and develop a progression of mastery exercises with each additional step requiring just a bit more effort than the previous step.

4. **Encourage Goal-Setting and Charting**: People tend to do what gets measured. Ask players to write down season goals and have them chart progress. For example, teach the reverse lay-up and have them shoot 10–15 each practice. Have them keep track of how many they make each day. Carry the charts with you to each practice and have them fill them in after they take their shots. Encourage

them to compete with themselves rather than with team-mates.

5. **Desensitize Them to Pressure**: The greater part of courage is having done a thing before. The second time we face a challenge, it is less scary.

Give athletes experiences with pressure situations at practice. Shoot free throws in practice when they are tired (as in games) with a consequence to simulate game pressure. Have players shoot free throws with everyone on the team running a wind sprint or doing five push-ups if the shooter misses. This will help players learn to deal with the pressure that a game brings.

6. **Be Influence-able**: It is lack of control—not the task itself—that overwhelms us. People with ways to cope and who believe a situation is manageable do not become stressed out.

You are an important part of an athlete's environment. If your players believe they have influence with you, their sense of control over their environment will be increased. Listen to them. Solicit their ideas about how the team can deal with problems and improve. Implement their advice as much as possible.

What Coaches Can't Do

I have seen coaches and parents determined to make their kids into superstars. Tragically, they often have the reverse effect. You can't make kids into superstars. You can only nurture their development as great competitors. The athlete has to want it more than you want it, or it's not going to happen.

So relax. Nurture the characteristics of great competitors in *all* your athletes. Ultimately it's up to them. That's the way it works.

PCA offers a workshop for high-school coaches, *Developing Triple-Impact Competitors,* that defines a competitor as someone who is committed to making oneself better, one's teammates better, and the game itself better. Info at **www.positivecoach.org**.

Chapter 13

Helping Individuals Become a Team

Too often the idealized profile of a coach is a genius who directs his players like puppets. A more suitable ideal: someone who unlocks the capabilities of a group of people.

Better Than They Should Have to Be

Taylor Branch, author of *Parting the Waters*, and other books about Martin Luther King, Jr., said that leadership often requires followers to be "better than they should have to be." When your team plays a more talented team to a standstill for an entire game, it shouldn't have to play an overtime session at an even higher level. But coaching leadership can and should ask them to try.

Leadership often demands commitments from followers greater than the followers believe they are capable of making. Asking your players to achieve excellence, to become more than they believe they are capable of, is a crucial step in developing a high-performance team.

I am talking here **not** about coaches browbeating kids into performing for the benefit of adults. I am talking about inspiring players as a group to reach for the stars; *asking* them to make a commitment to achieve a level of performance that most groups rarely experience: in short, to become a team. But to do that successfully it helps to understand what keeps them from doing that.

Self-Protection Strategies

Groups are dangerous. Even children realize the power a group has. Groups can make people do things they don't want to do. Groups can embarrass and take advantage of people. When we join a group, we try to protect ourselves. We worry about protecting ourselves until we are convinced the group will not hurt us. There are four self-protection strategies individuals use when entering a new group.

1. **"Fight"**: Some people respond to the anxiety that comes with uncertainty by trying to organize things. They face the threat by becoming aggressive and bossy. Fight-response athletes may give directions for things they themselves don't know how to do correctly. The anxiety tied to the ambiguity of the situation drives them to take charge regardless of their competency to do so.

Organizing energy when it is focused on the needs of the team is great. When the principal motivation is self-protection, it often will be counterproductive.

2. **"Flight"**: At the other extreme, many of us lie low and get the lay of the land before committing to anything that might make us too vulnerable. I tend to take my time in a new group, testing the waters to see how people respond if I disagree with them. Once I am convinced the group is safe, I become a vocal, enthusiastic member.

As with Fight behaviors, it is useful for groups to have Flight people who look before they leap. But if the goal of the lying-low person is self-protection rather than advancement of the group toward its goals, the individual may not speak out when the group needs to hear what she has to say.

3. **Alliance-Builder**: A self-protection strategy related to the lie-low approach is to look for individuals within the group to ally with. If I support someone, perhaps they'll support me if anyone criticizes me. Thus my goal is not to make the group successful, but to find a friend or two who will protect me.

4. **Scapegoating**: The most insidious self-protection strategy is to seek a scapegoat to blame for the problems of the group. If we can blame everything on someone else, no one will think to blame us. Or, if they do, we may be able to shift the blame to the scapegoat.

Some coaches try to create a common enemy outside the team. But resorting to external enemies to motivate a team can backfire. The negative emotion brought into play can detract from concentration and overall performance. And, if you don't defeat the external opponent, the bitter feelings return with the group seeking a scapegoat for the loss.

Often a scapegoat is someone who is a little (or a lot) different. It may be the weakest player or an athlete from the "wrong side of the tracks," or someone who wears weird clothes. And, of course, often the scapegoat is someone from a minority group (a lone girl on a co-ed team, the only athlete of color, etc.).

Scapegoats often "nominate" themselves. The athlete may have habits that bug the coach or teammates. She may not seem to try as hard as others on the team. He may fail to make a key play that other players could make with ease.

The bottom line is scapegoats distract people from doing the hard work of trying to get better. It's much easier to blame some poor soul for the failure of the team. If it's "his" fault, then "we" don't have to take responsibility for working harder to get better.

Your players will engage in self-protection strategies *until* they have confidence that the team will not harm them. When your players and coaches reach this level of confidence, you have the potential to become a team in more than name only.

The Requirements of a Successful Team

A new group goes through a sorting out process before it becomes a team working together for a common goal. Four general requirements must be satisfied in the minds of your players and coaches before they can become a real team.

1. **Acceptance**: Each player must feel accepted by her coaches and teammates before she can devote anything close to 100% of her energies to helping her team win. You can often tell watching practice which players feel they aren't on an equal footing with the others.

2. **Influence**: All groups demand something from their members. If I think a team or coach is going to make me do something harmful, or against my values, I will never stop looking over my shoulder. Once I believe I can influence

what happens to me on this team, then I can throw myself wholeheartedly into helping the team win. Without influence I will spend much of my energy worrying rather than working to make the team better. (The tools in Chapter 4 on influence-ability and listening are especially useful for this.)

3. **Identity**: Am I an important member of the group or am I on the team because they need a certain number of players? Do I have a role that will help the team achieve its goals? If I feel like I do, I will be able to focus on helping the team be successful. If I don't, I may actually be happier when the team fails.

4. **Goal Matching**: Each player needs to feel that he wins if the team wins. Here, applying terms from *Strategic Selling* by Robert Miller and Steven Heiman, the difference between a "result" and a "win" is important to understand. A result is something that is good for the organization, e.g., winning a game. A "win" is something that is good for the individual player, e.g., getting more playing time or getting public credit for helping the team win.

Often coaches fail to ask what would be a win for each player. A basketball team may benefit by its point guard passing more and shooting less. But if the point guard gets his internal goodies from scoring, the coach would do well to figure out how to convince him that he will benefit more if the team wins, even if that means fewer points.

Ask each of your players about their individual and team goals. Asking players what goals they have to help their teammates (and the team) succeed sends a message that this is important to you and the team culture.

Liking Versus Caring

It's rare in any group for everyone to like each other. Some players will be best buddies, and some just won't click with each other. Some players may dislike each other, particularly if they are competing with each other for playing time.

I explain to my players the difference between liking and caring. I tell players that I don't expect them to all like each other. In a sense liking someone is involuntary. You either do or you don't, at least initially. But caring is an act of will. You can *decide* that you are going to act in ways to help another person (which is what caring is) even if you don't particularly like them. That is the standard I ask my players to aspire to: acting in ways that show we care about each other.

The Portable Home Team Advantage

I ask my players why the home team wins so often. Usually they come up with answers like having the home crowd rooting for them causes players to try harder and play with more confidence. Then I say that we can create a **portable** home team advantage we can take with us wherever we play.

On most teams, when a player makes a mistake, other players will criticize her. By supporting each other, by saying things like, "It's okay to make a mistake," or "Nice try, now focus on the next play," we can create an atmosphere where we do better because we become our own home court advantage.

Awards That Undermine Team Spirit

There is an old saying, "It's amazing how much you can get done when it doesn't matter who gets the credit." The reverse is also true. It's depressing how little gets done when people focus on who gets the credit.

Team spirit can be fractured by the selection of the most valuable player or other awards that allocate credit for a team's success. Instead of giving pro-style awards, consider giving personalized awards that address the unique contribution each player made to the team. See Chapter 15 for examples of awards that contribute to team spirit rather than undercut it.

The Ultimate Coaching High: Beating Better Talent

There are few things in life more exciting that watching a high functioning team in action. It's even more exciting when you are part of that team, as a player or coach. Occasionally in my years of coaching, things have clicked and the individual players have become a unit, functioning as if with a common brain.

My favorite situation as a coach is to have a team that is a little bit weaker than the better teams in the league. I often wonder at coaches who work so hard to get the most talented players on their team, and then win every game by a wide margin. What challenge is there in that?

On the other hand, I relish facing a team with better talent because it gives us the chance to rise to the challenge—as a coach, as individual players, and as a team. In this situation, even losing can be a triumph when you play over your head and come much closer to winning than anyone (except you and your players) would ever have thought you could.

And when you win, it provides a feeling of deep satisfaction for each member of the team. It means that you have realized the ultimate for a coach: you've created a *team*, an organism greater than the sum of the individual parts.

PCA offers a workshop on creating team culture that inspires players to give their best. Information on the *Double-Goal Coach: Culture, Practices, and Games* workshop can be found at **www.positivecoach.org** or by calling 1-866-725-0024 (toll-free).

Chapter 14

Coaching the Special Kids

What makes a kid special is attention by an important adult in his or her life. For an athlete, the coach is a very important adult indeed.

Coaching kids who are similar in age, ability and background is challenging. When one or more of the kids are special in an important way, it can get complicated.

The Superstar

Coaches love to have a superstar on their team—you can almost see coaches drool at tryouts when a talented player shows up. Here's how to maximize the team experience when you have a superstar.

- **The Placeholder Effect**: It's natural to go to a superstar in crunch time. This causes the rest of team to become placeholders rather than aggressively trying to make plays to win games. Tell players they all need to make plays! Call plays for other players in crunch time to make them believe you.

- **No Special Treatment**: Don't give superstars special treat-ment. It hurts the team and it hurts them. Other players may think if you have talent, you don't have to follow the rules. It becomes hard for a superstar to develop the attitude and work habits that will allow him to excel at the elite level (where everyone has talent) if he begins to think of himself as being above team rules.

- **Being a Leader**: A leader is someone who makes her teammates better and more effective. Tell your superstar early and often that she needs to be a leader, which means bringing out the best in teammates. Make sure she knows how to fill the E-Tanks of her teammates and ask her to do it.

- **Self-Handicapping**: Encourage your superstar to make things more challenging by self-handicapping. Ask him to use only his weak hand or foot for an entire practice session, for example. Everyone gets more excited by "just-right challenges." Ask him to do what he needs to do to create one for himself.

The Big Kid

Some kids mature early. If you have a big kid, avoid the temptation to limit him to "big" positions—lineman in football, under the basket in basketball. Many big kids end up being normal-sized when they mature, and you can do them a big favor by having them learn positions and skills that don't rely on size for success.

The Weak Athlete

I have a special place in my heart for the athlete who competes though it doesn't come easy. Coaches can have a huge positive impact with weaker athletes. And games are often won or lost by the actions of weaker players. Make sure your weaker players have fun. If they have fun, they'll keep coming back. And help them *see themselves as improving!* Learning new skills is fun. Take time to help weak athletes improve and recognize that they are improving. These two things will keep them in the game, and you never know—your weak athlete may be a late bloomer who becomes a star as she matures.

The Child with Behavior Problems

Every coach runs into kids who misbehave. Here are three principles for dealing with behavior problems:

1. **Reinforce behavior you want**: Attention, good or bad, can reinforce behavior you don't want. As strange as it may seem, yelling at a kid can be reinforcing. Give your attention to the kids who do what you want them to do. If all your players come in when you call except one, thank the kids who come right away: "Billy, Tommy, Steve, thanks for hustling in here!"

2. **Ignore behavior you don't want**: Justin didn't come when you called, so ignore him. Until he does what you want, Justin doesn't exist (actually you keep an eye on him so he doesn't get hurt without him knowing it). When Justin realizes he can't get your attention by misbehaving, he'll likely try to get it by complying. When he does, reward him with your attention: "Justin, thanks for doing what I asked you!" This tends to work like magic, but not always, so read on.

3. **When you can't ignore**: Sometimes you can't ignore a player's behavior—she may be putting herself in danger or

disrupting your practice. Here you intervene in a "least-at-tention manner." "Sarah, I need you to sit over here until you can follow my directions. As soon as you are ready to do what I ask, you can rejoin the team." If this doesn't work, add a check-in. "Sarah, you sit here until I come back. Think about whether you can do as I ask. I'll be back shortly to see if you are ready to rejoin the team." This is a good time for a fun team activity that Sarah will miss. When you return, have her acknowledge what she needs to do before she can rejoin the team. "Sarah, are you able to follow my direction now?" Sarah has to agree before you let her rejoin the team.

These principles are simple but not easy. We get angry when a child misbehaves and it feels unnatural to ignore misbehavior. But they work. Try them and see.

The Hard-to-Like Kid

Every coach has, from time to time, a player he just doesn't click with. When you have a player you find it hard to like, here's what you do: ***Act as if***. You *act as if* you like the kid. Check out the E-Tank filling ideas in Chapter 4 and then use as many of them as you can with this youth. If you continu-ously act like you like a player, it is pretty much guaranteed that you will begin to like him.

The "Solo" Athlete

Being the "only" on a team is stressful. Solo status can be a girl on a boys' team, an ethnic minority on a white team, a poor kid at an elite private school, etc. The best way to address this is to get another solo or two on the team so the solo is no longer a solo. If one girl is on your team, recruit another. If your league has two girls, having them together on one team is better for them than putting them on different teams. If you can't do this, then make sure the solo feels wanted by you. Ask your best players to help fill the E-Tank of the solo athlete.

Children with Handicaps

Children with handicaps are a particular kind of solo case. Having an athlete with a handicap on your team can be a fantastic growth opportunity for him and for his teammates—one that kids are likely to say was the highlight of the season if handled well. Some tips to maximize the experience for an athlete with a handicap.

- **Proper Positioning**: Find a position where the player can have the most chance for success. Help him understand the basic requirements of the position including where to position himself.

- **Multiple Teaching Modes**: All kids benefit from a 1-2-3 of 1) telling, 2) showing, 3) walking through, but an athlete with handicaps especially so. I've had success walking through a play with my hands on the player's back so he gets the feel of the play.

- **Special Plays**: Create a special play for your special athlete, for example, in basketball a double pick to open him up for a lay-up or a three-point shot. Not only does this create excitement for him, but the rest of the team will enjoy helping him get his moment to shine. It also adds incentive for him to work on his shooting so as to be ready when his play is called.

- **Recruit other athletes with handicaps**: As with any solo, having others like her will help the athlete with a handicap, so see if you can get other similar athletes on your and other teams in the league.

- **Get Advice**: Find out the agency in your area that has expertise with your player's issues and call to get a consultation. They may also be able to help you find other players similar to yours who you can recruit for your team or league.

Many innovative programs exist around the country. Boca Hoops in Boca Raton, FL, a winner of PCA's national *Honoring the Game Award*, has created "High-Five Basketball" for youth with disabilities (http://www.high5basketball.org/). Depending on the disability, you will find many resources including Special Olympics and government agencies dealing with individuals and families with disabilities. Information and nomination forms for PCA's National Youth Sports Awards which annually honor coaches and youth sports organizations is at www.positivecoach.org.

The Sibling in the Shadow

It's tough to follow a sibling who was a great athlete. Many excellent athletes seem disappointing because they aren't as good as their sibling. If you have a sibling in the shadow, shine the light on her. Act as if you have never heard of the older sibling. If someone else refers to how good the sibling was, tell your player that what you expect from him is that he try his hardest and have fun playing the game. And that you are glad **he** is on your team!

The Scapegoat

A repeating tragedy in life is the search for a scapegoat when things go wrong. Likely scapegoat candidates include the child who is not so likable or the weakest player or one who is different, perhaps a solo. Recognize that scapegoats are a way of avoiding the hard work of trying to achieve excellence. When you see someone becoming a scapegoat, stick up for her! Tell whoever is blaming her for the problems of the team, that you like having her on your team and point out contributions she's made. A player of yours can't be a scapegoat if you defend her.

Specializing the Unspecial Kids

Most kids aren't superstars or big kids or siblings-in-the-shadow, etc. Most kids are "unspecial" by most definitions. They don't excel and they don't cause much of a problem. They're there but they go unnoticed. That is a shame, because every child is special. Your players will all be special when you give them special treatment. When you begin to see each of them as special, they will be!

Chapter 15

Ending the Season With a Bang

Going through a season with a team of youth athletes is a truck-load of highs and lows. Completing a season is worth celebrating, whether your team ended up as champions or in last place!

The End-of-the-Season Party

A team party allows you to put the season into perspective while reinforcing the life lessons you have emphasized all season. Find a suitable place for the party where people can hear each other. Noisy pizza parlors, unless they have a separate room or an out-of-the-way area, may not be the best place.

Recognizing Your Players

Make sure that *every* player gets recognized for her accomplishments and contributions during the season. If you have been doing Positive Charting (see Chapter 1), you will have plenty of material to use for this.

Personalized Awards

Awards that mimic professional sports (e.g., "Most Valuable Player") can leave players resentful if they think they deserved the award more than the recipient. Instead, create awards for each athlete that expresses his unique contributions during the season.

You can use playing cards of professional players or create a special certificate for each player with a specific award name that recognizes that player. For example:

- *The Play-Anywhere Award* for being willing to play wherever you needed her without complaint.

- *Mr. Reliable Award* for consistently playing hard throughout the season.

- *The Mental Toughness Award* for bouncing back from adversity.

- *The Cardiac Arrest Award* for making outfield catches that left the coaches in need of pacemakers.

- *Mr. Clutch Award* for making big plays when the team needed them.

Teachable Moments After the Season

Kids pay attention when you are talk about them at the end-of-season party, so make the most of this teachable moment. It's also a chance to communicate with parents because you can bet they are listening to your comments about their child. Plan a party that ends the season with a bang. Even (or especially!) if it has been a tough season when things did not go as hoped. End the season by endorsing each player to help him feel great about himself and the season he just completed.

Chapter 16

Every Kid a Coach!

Few of your players will be stars on high school or college (let alone professional) teams. But most will get married and have kids. And every one of them can become a great coach who will pass on the lessons they learned from you.

The Goal: Every Kid a Coach

Coaching involves communication, encouragement, teaching, developing strong relationships and learning to motivate a group of people to accomplish great things. These skills are relevant to any career your athletes pursue. Give your players an edge: help them become effective coaches.

The Lasting Impact of Positive Coaching

Most of us want to leave an impact, to be remembered for having done something of lasting importance. There is no better way than Positive Coaching to do that.

Be the Coach You Would've Wanted to Play For

Sometimes in coaching workshops, I ask coaches to describe the best coach they ever had. Their stories are wonderful and poignant, often about coaches who are long dead. They describe coaches who were wise, encouraging, gentle, disciplined, great teachers, and wonderful human beings who cared about them as individuals, as well as athletes.

Tara VanDerveer, Stanford University's women's basketball coach, once told me that her goal was to "be the kind of coach I would have wanted to play for."

So, I end this book with two challenges and wishes for you in your great adventure as a coach of young people.

1. Set a goal to turn each player into a coach who will pass on what you are teaching them about life and sports.

2. Remember what you wanted in a coach when you were young, and do everything in your power to become the coach that you would have wanted to play for.

Go for it! You and your players deserve it!

Positive Coaching Alliance (**www.positivecoach.org**) is about giving every athlete a positive coach. If you are excited about PCA's mission, become a member. Encourage your league to partner with PCA. Contact PCA at 1-866-725-0024 (toll-free) or at pca@positivecoach.org.

Things I want to remember